MW00986069

THE TEACHINGS OF
Seventh-day Adventism

THE TEACHINGS OF

Seventh-day Adventism

John H. Gerstner

BAKER BOOK HOUSE
Grand Rapids, Michigan 49516

Copyright © 1960 by Baker Books
a division of Baker Book House Company
P.O. Box 6287, Grand Rapids, MI 49516-6287

Originally appeared as chapter two and appendix in
The Theology of the Major Sects

ISBN: 0-8010-3720-4

Seventeenth printing, June 2003

Printed in the United States of America

For information about academic books, resources for
Christian leaders, and all new releases available from
Baker Book House, visit our web site:
http://www.bakerbooks.com/

Contents

Introduction

The abundance of literature on various "sects" shows that there is great interest in the subject. But what is a *sect?* We must make our definition clear, for there is wide difference of opinion on its meaning.

Evangelicals generally use *sect* when referring to those denominations which do not hold to fundamental biblical principles—especially the deity of Christ and His atonement. This booklet is written from the evangelical perspective.

The Teachings of Seventh-day Adventism is designed as a ready reference booklet. It is meant to be a quick guide to the wealth of literature on this subject, and it includes a valuable table and glossary.

The general exposition in the first chapter gives an easily-grasped overview of the sect. The following chapter, "Doctrines of Seventh-day Adventists," provides the reference material which summarizes the first chapter and adds some more technical data. Chapter two contains the basic theological structure of Seventh-day Adventists, stated objectively and concisely. The text itself gives a fuller exposition of some of the cardinal points outlined in the first chapter.

Chapter three, "Terms Frequently Used by Seventh-day Adventists," gives some of the most common terms in the vocabulary of this sect. Sects often have their own precise definitions for common religious words, and the glossary makes this immediately evident.

Chapter four, "For Further Reading," lists both primary and secondary sources for further study of the theology and practice of the sect.

A summary of the essential teachings of traditional Christianity appears in chapter five. This summary is included to provide a basis for comparison with the doctrines of Seventh-day Adventists. This chapter is designed to be used as a frame of reference.

To make the theologies of different sects clearer, their teachings have been summarized in the "Chart of Comparative Doctrines" at the end of chapter six. This tabular outline classifies the doctrines of each group in relation to the tenets of orthodox Christianity. Beginning with the doctrines of the Seventh-day Adventists, and continuing with the teachings of the Jehovah's Witnesses, Mormons, and Christian Scientists, this chart allows the reader to see at a glance the position of each group on various Christian doctrines.

1 Description and History of Seventh-day Adventism*

In the mid-nineteenth century, feelings that men were experiencing the Last Days were rife:

> This was the grand clue—of the seventy weeks as the first segment of the 2300 years, cut off for the Jews and climaxing with the Messiah—that burst simultaneously upon the minds of men in Europe and America, and even in Asia and Africa. This was the great advance truth that led to the emphasis upon the 2300 years from 457 B.C. to A.D. 1843 or 1844 which we have surveyed. Clearer and clearer became the perception in the first four decades of the nineteenth century, until it reached its peak in America in the summer and autumn of 1844, contemporaneously with the predicted time of the prophecy.[1]

This is the historical setting which the outstanding Adventist scholar, Leroy Froom, in his massive and erudite volumes of *The Prophetic Faith of Our Fathers,* finds for the work of William Miller, whom he seems to regard as the first of the Adventists. Sears in *Days of Delusion,* Minnigerode in *The Fabulous Forties,* and others also seemed aware of the fact that "In no other period in American history were 'the last days' felt to be so imminent as in that between 1820 and 1845."[2] Froom's work shows us that this phenomenon was by no means restricted to this continent.

William Miller

It was on the crest of this eschatological wave that William Miller was borne, and in its trough Seventh-day Adventism followed. Miller was born in Pittsfield, Massachusetts, on February 15, 1782. A reputable farmer, good soldier, and captain in the War of 1812, and apparently an outstanding citizen, he did not become famous until religious vicissitudes led him to a closer study of the Scriptures. At first, he was a rather typical, earnest member of the local Baptist church, but some skeptical friends of his eventually swept him into a frigid deism. After he had found his religious faith again, he applied himself much more earnestly to the study of the Bible. (Some would say that he applied himself too earnestly.) This pious farmer utilized

---

*There may be a difference of opinion as to whether the Seventh-day Adventists should be classified as a "sect." Dr. Walter Martin classifies them as an evangelical group and makes a strong case for his view in his book, *The Truth About Seventh-day Adventism.* We would urge all interested students to secure Dr. Martin's book and reread this booklet in the light of that book.

[1] L. E. Froom, *Prophetic Faith of Our Fathers,* Vol. III, p. 749.
[2] Fawn Brodie, *No Man Knows My History,* p. 101.

every spare moment for sixteen years with his Bible and his concordance. Still, it is understandable that such a person, being unprotected by the corrective of church tradition, might very well fall into some naive and extreme notions. Miller showed admirable restraint when, feeling that he had made a great discovery of the very imminent return of his Lord, he was still able to say:

> My great fear was, that in their joy at the hope of a glorious inheritance so soon to be revealed, they would receive the doctrine without sufficiently examining the Scriptures in demonstration of its truth. I therefore feared to present it, lest by some possibility I should be in error, and be the means of misleading any.[3]

Still, one wonders why this untrained farmer did not hesitate to take the platform and announce to the world with bold certainty the outcome of his calculations about obscure prophetic predictions. As William Biederwolf said, "He was as ignorant of Hebrew as a Hottentot is of the Klondyke." That fact could have given him some reason for holding back from *ex cathedra* deliverances about the meaning of the 2300 days that are not supposed to be days and the seventy weeks that are not weeks. But after being asked to speak at a little church in Dresden, and there to continue for a week of services, it was not long before Miller was writing to his friend, Hendryx, "I devote my whole time, lecturing."[4]

The Growth of Adventism

By 1840 Adventism was becoming a significant religious movement. It was in that year that the influential Adventist periodical, *The Signs of the Times,* made its appearance to spread the imminency message far and wide. But more important still, the number of preachers and lecturers of the rousing message that Christ was due to return in 1843 had so increased that they quite naturally began a loose organization—always the first step toward a new sect. On October 13, 1840, a conference was held at the Reverend Joshua V. Himes' Chardon Street Chapel, Boston. Great camp meetings began to characterize the ever-widening reach of the Adventist push.

Finally, the great year of Millerite expectation, March 21, 1842 to March 21, 1843, came and went, but Christ was nowhere to be seen. Miller waited in vain—a disappointed man aware that he had made a mistake but was incapable of finding it. Six weeks later he wrote to his disillusioned followers:

> Were I to live my life over again, with the same evidence that I then had, to be honest with God and man I should have to do as I have done. Although

[3]William Miller, *Apology and Defense,* p. 16, cited by Francis D. Nichol, *Midnight Cry,* p. 34.
[4]Nichol, *Midnight Cry,* p. 57.

opposers said it would not come, they produced no weighty arguments. It was evidently guesswork with them; and I then thought, and do now, that their denial was based more on an unwillingness for the Lord to come than on any arguments leading to such a conclusion. [This was a most uncharitable remark, for many of these critics were lovers of the Lord and His glorious appearing who simply did not expect Him in 1843.] I *confess my error,* and acknowledge *my disappointment;* yet I still believe that the day of the Lord is near, even at the door; and I exhort you, my brethren, to be watchful, and not let that day come upon you unawares.[5]

Millerite hopes were now down but not out. 1844 dragged on flatly. Meetings went on flatly. At Exeter, New Hampshire, on August 12th, a camp meeting was dragging on when, rather suddenly, as if driven by the silent demand of a grieving multitude, one of the brothers announced that the return of Christ would be in the seventh month of the current Jewish year. The proposal caught on. The fading hopes lived again. A fixed date was set and once again, more fervently than ever before, the Millerites set out to warn the world; only this time Miller was to catch the fire rather than start it. October 22: The end of the world!

In ten weeks the great day was at hand. In a Philadelphia store window the following sign was displayed: "This shop is closed in honor of the King of kings, who will appear about the 20th of October. Get ready, friends, to crown Him Lord of all."[6] A group of two hundred left the city, just as Lot had left Sodom before impending doom. Most of the Millerites gave up their occupations during the last days; farmers left their crops in the fields. But the usual meetings in which the believers gathered were surprisingly orderly and free of fanaticism. The sober Adventist research reveals that the stories of Millerites climbing up mountains and poles and clothing themselves in white ascension robes were tall tales; the charges of adventist insanity are reversed by sober, critical investigation.[7] Be all this as it may, the excitement was naturally very great and the second disappointment shattering.

But hope seemed to spring eternal among the Adventists. Their basic Christian faith would not be crushed. And though they were no longer adjusting their timetable for the Lord's return, they did keep their adventist hope alive. In April 29, 1845, they assembled at Albany to take inventory of their hopes and state their faith. This meeting held them together.

Five years after Christ did not come to Miller, Miller went to be with Christ. "At the time appointed," his tombstone at Low Hampton reads, "the end shall be."

---

[5]Bliss, *Memoirs of William Miller,* p. 256, cited by Nichol, *Midnight Cry,* p. 171.
[6]Cf. Nichol, *Midnight Cry,* pp. 238 ff., 362f., 413.
[7]Cf. Francis D. Nichol, "The Growth of the Millerite Legend" in *Church History,* vol. XXI, no. 4, December, 1952, pp. 296 ff.

Mrs. Ellen G. White

Miller was succeeded in the leadership of the Adventist movement by a person who was in every respect different from him. One obvious difference was that she was a woman—Mrs. Ellen G. White. She was a visionary where Miller had been a rather sober student. Miller always attempted to ground his witness on his exposition of the Bible, but Mrs. White went beyond the Bible with her numerous "revelations." When Miller was mistaken he admitted it, but Mrs. White denied any error. While Miller was frankly disappointed, Mrs. White turned defeat into victory by reinterpretation.

Her very first vision was the cue: in 1844 right after the grand disillusionment, Mrs. White "saw" the Adventists marching straight to heaven. Mrs. White had a job for life as seer, and the Adventists had new assurance. Until her death in 1915, she was the outstanding Adventist leader. And, judging from Jan Van Baalen's remark, though her teachings sometimes cause embarrassment, she still holds sway:

> . . . it will not do for officials of this church to invite the present writer to forget about Mrs. White and to read current S.D.A. publications, while these same current publications state, "For her emphasis of Bible truth, for her application of specific doctrines, for her simplification of the deep things of God . . . the S.D.A. denomination and the world in general owe a great debt to Ellen G. White."[8]

The Theology of Seventh-day Adventism

There is every indication that Seventh-day Adventism holds many of the catholic Christian doctrines. Miller, for example, in 1822 wrote a brief creed. As Francis Nichol says, "Any Calvinistic Baptist would probably subscribe to all except one of them, with scarcely a change of a word. In fact, if we eliminate from his creed Calvin's dour doctrine of predestination, and the Baptist statement on the mode of baptism, virtually all conservative Protestant bodies would subscribe to the views he set down."[9] Later Seventh-day Adventists have done very little to alter these views: they have merely modified Miller somewhat, held to the general Arminian system, and added several distinctive positions (especially pertaining to the atonement, the Sabbath, and the future).

The Adventists accept the inspiration and authority of the Bible. Unfortunately, they also virtually accept the inspiration and authority of Mrs. Ellen G. White. As a matter of fact, it seems highly doubtful that the Seventh-day Adventists would ever have come into existence but for the notion that in 1844 Christ entered into the heavenly sanctuary, and they could never have become sure of such an idea

---

[8]Jan Karel Van Baalen, *The Chaos of Cults*, 1956 edition, p. 224.
[9]Nichol, *Midnight Cry*, p. 36.

without the visions of Mrs. White. The Adventists held their prophetess in high esteem. Biederwolf, however, was not so impressed by her abilities as a seeress. He lists a long number of unfulfilled visions, such as the following:

> In one of her visions her accompanying angels told her that the time of salvation for all sinners ended in 1844. She now claims the door of mercy is still open.
>
> In another vision she discovered that women should wear short dresses with pants and she and her sister followers dressed this way for eight years. But the ridiculous custom has now been abandoned. . . .[10]

It is not in the realm of theology that Adventism deviates so greatly from the catholic Christian tradition, nor with respect to the person of Christ, but in its view of the atonement. " 'We dissent,' they say, 'from the view that the atonement was made upon the cross as is generally held.' "[11] The atonement was begun then but it was not ended then. For, "by a life of perfect obedience and by His sacrificial death, He satisfied divine justice, and made *provision for* atonement for the sins of men. . . ."[12] Christ's work as an atoning priest, according to Adventists, is not yet complete. He has yet to make the great atonement for sins. The formal blotting out of sins is still in the future. What delays Him? What is He doing now? In 1844 He entered the heavenly sanctuary and presumably is still there. He will complete the atonement when He comes out of the sanctuary and lays the sins of His people on Satan, who, like ancient Azazel, bears them away forever.

Adventists hold to a rigorous system of sanctification in which a strict conformity to divine commands is appropriately enjoined. Characteristic of the group is an Old Testament legal flavor to their laws. This is undoubtedly an outgrowth of their vigorous defense of the Jewish Saturday as the continuing Christian Sabbath. In their eagerness to show that the law is still binding, there is a proportionately high regard for other Old Testament laws (generally thought by other Christians to be abrogated).

The following reasons refute the Adventist insistence on the perpetual obligation to observe the Lord's Day on Saturday. *First,* although the Sabbath Day is perpetually binding as a part of the moral law, it does not follow that ancient legal features of that day are likewise necessarily binding—certainly not if there is evidence that they have been altered by later revelation. The particular day of the week is surely unimportant. A seventh day may be essential, but *which* seventh day could not possibly be essential. Just as Saturday

---

[10]Biederwolf, *Seventh-Day Adventism,* pp. 8f.

[11]*Fundamental Principles* (S.D.A. tract), p. 2, cited by Biederwolf, *Seventh-Day Adventism,* p. 24.

[12]*What Do Seventh-Day Adventists Believe?* (S.D.A. tract), p. 6, cited by Van Baalen, *Chaos of Cults,* p. 173.

could have originally been most appropriate as symbolic of the day of rest after creation, so Sunday could later become most appropriate as the day of rest after redemption. The Hebrew word for "Sabbath" means "rest," not "Saturday." Saturday was shown to be the intended Sabbath, when God gave a double portion of manna on the preceding day. In the new dispensation Sunday was shown to be the intended Sabbath when God raised His Son on that day.

Second, the New Testament does indicate that just such a change was made. Christ arose on Sunday, appeared on Sunday, the disciples assembled on Sunday, offerings were made on Sunday, and John was in the Spirit on Sunday.

The *third* reason grows out of the second and serves as a distinct confirmation of it. The practice of the early church revealed an early observation of Sunday as the new Sabbath, although the old Sabbath was observed when the church was still a part of Israel. Biederwolf has conveniently gathered the statements from the early Fathers:

The *Epistle of Barnabas* (A.D. 100) says, "Wherefore also we keep the eighth day with joyfulness, the day also on which Jesus rose from the dead."

The *Epistles of Ignatius* (A.D. 107), a pupil of the apostles whose writings were commended by Polycarp, a friend of St. John's, says: "And after the observance of the Sabbath, let every friend of Christ keep the Lord's day as a festival, the resurrection day, the queen and chief of all days.

"Those who were concerned with old things have come to newness of confidence, no longer keeping Sabbaths, but living according to the Lord's day, on which our life as risen again through Him depends."

In the writings of *Justin Martyr* (A.D. 145), it is said, "But Sunday is the day on which we all hold our common assembly, because it is the first day of the week and Jesus Christ our Saviour on the same day rose from the dead."

For some time Jewish Christians continued to keep both the Sabbath and Sunday, but according to Justin Martyr such believers were to be accommodated as weak brothers. He says in his *Dialogue* with Trypho, chapter 47: "But if some, through weakmindedness, wish to observe such institutions as were given by Moses, along with their hope in Christ, yet choose to live with the Christians and the faithful, as I said before, not inducing them either to be circumcised, like themselves, or to keep the Sabbath, or to observe any other such ceremonies, then I hold that we ought to join ourselves to such, and associate with them in all things as kinsmen and brethren."

Apostolic Constitutions (Second Century): "On the day of the resurrection of the Lord, that is, the Lord's day, assemble yourselves together without fail, giving thanks to God and praising Him for those mercies God has bestowed upon you through Christ."

Dionysius of Corinth (A.D. 170), in an epistle to the Church of Rome, wrote: "Today we kept the Lord's holy day in which we read your letter."

Melito of Sardis (A.D. 175) wrote a treatise on "The Lord's Day."

Irenaeus (A.D. 160–200) says: "The mystery of the Lord's resurrection may not be celebrated on any other day than the Lord's Day and on this alone should we observe the breaking of the Paschal Feast."

Clement of Alexandria (A.D. 174) says: "The old seventh day has become nothing more than a working day."

Bardesanes (A.D. 180) says in his book of the *Laws of the Countries,* "On one day, the first of the week, we assemble ourselves together."

Tertullian (A.D. 200) says in his *Apologeticus:* "In the same way if we devote Sunday to rejoicing, from a far different reason than sun-worship, we have some resemblance to some of you 'The Jews,' who devote the day of Saturn [Saturday] to ease and luxury." In another of his works he says: "He who argues for Sabbath keeping and circumcision must show that Adam and Abel and the just of old times observed these things. . . . We observe the day of the Lord's resurrection laying aside our worldly business."

Origen (A.D. 185–255) says: "John the Baptist was born to make ready a people for the Lord, a people fit for Him at the end of the Covenant now grown old, which is the end of the Sabbath." He further says, "It is one of the marks of a perfect Christian to keep the Lord's day."

Victorianus (A.D. 300) says: "On the Lord's day we go forth to our bread with the giving of thanks. Lest we should appear to observe any Sabbath with the Jews, which Christ himself the Lord of the Sabbath in his body abolished" (*On the Creation of the World,* section 14).

Peter, Bishop of Alexandria (A.D. 306), says: "But the Lord's day we celebrate as the day of joy because on it He rose again."

Eusebius (A.D. 324) of the Ebionites says: "They also observed the Sabbath and other discipline of the Jews just like them, but on the other hand, they also celebrate the Lord's Day very much like us" (*Ecclesiastical History,* pages 112f.).

A *fourth* argument is the inherently inconsistent position of the Adventists on the Saturday Sabbath. For one thing, they are obliged to abandon some of the strict Jewish regulations, such as the one forbidding the picking up of sticks to make a fire. Unfortunately, some Adventists actually regard all who observe Sunday as having received the mark of the beast.[13] They say that ". . . evangelical churches that do not observe the seventh day are 'the false

---

[13]Ellen G. White, *The Great Controversy,* 1911 ed., p. 449.

church'. . . ."[14] The United States government becomes a dragon when it makes Sabbath laws; the Adventists work earnestly against laws that protect the American Sunday.[15] One evangelist goes so far as to make refusal to observe Saturday the "unpardonable sin."[16]

This defensive spirit developed early in the movement when it was found that most of the evangelical churches were not sympathetic to the Millerite expectation. First, Fitch told Adventists of their obligation to come out of other churches, Protestant no less than Romanist.[17] This sentiment spread rapidly. But Miller himself was able to say as late as 1844: " 'I have not advised anyone to separate from the churches to which they may have belonged, unless their brethren cast them out, or deny them religious privileges. . . . I have never designed to make a new sect. . . .' "[18] Joshua Himes came over to the separatist viewpoint finally, but Miller held out, though rather silently, to the end. Present-day Adventism requires would-be members to confess that the "Seventh-day Adventist Church is 'the remnant church.' "[19] This remnant and only true church (as they say) practices baptism by immersion, observes the Lord's Supper, and follows a congregationalist organization.

Unquestionably, the outstanding distinctive of the Adventist church is its eschatology. Its doctrine of the intermediate state—soul sleep—it shares with some other sects. ("The state to which we are reduced by death is one of silence, inactivity and entire unconsciousness."[20]) But, its doctrine of the Second Coming is uniquely its own. After Miller was disappointed in 1843 and again in 1844, one of the Adventists, Hiram Edson, claimed a vision of Christ entering the heavenly sanctuary. So Christ *had* returned—only not to earth, but to heaven. Mrs. White later gave this vision her imprimatur and filled out the various details.

How did the Adventists conclude that Christ would return in 1844? Basically they accepted Miller's calculations. Miller reasoned this way: Daniel 8:14 says that the sanctuary would be restored in "two thousand and three hundred days." Miller believed that a prophetic day equals one year. So he calculated that it was two thousand and three hundred years before the sanctuary was to be cleansed by Christ's return. But what was the date from which we are to calculate? Miller saw that there was the seventy weeks' passage in Daniel 9. He figured this meant seventy weeks of years; that is, seventy times seven years or four hundred ninety years. Four hundred ninety years, the

[14]"Are You on the Right Bus?" in *Signs of the Times,* Nov., 1945, cited by Van Baalen, *Chaos of Cults,* 1956 edition, p. 229.
[15]Blakely, *American State Papers on Freedom,* pp. 260 ff. and *passim.*
[16]Cf. Van Baalen, *Chaos of Cults,* 1956 edition, p. 229.
[17]Nichol, *Midnight Cry,* p. 148.
[18]*Signs of the Times,* Jan. 31, 1844, cited by Nichol, *Midnight Cry,* pp. 159f.
[19]Cf. Van Baalen, *Chaos of Cults,* 1956 edition, p. 229.
[20]*Fundamental Principles,* p. 12.

prophecy said, until the Messiah be cut off. When was Christ cut off? A.D. 33. Four hundred ninety years earlier brought us to the date 457 B.C., and that was the date of the determination of the decree allowing Ezra to return. Now add to this date the twenty-three hundred years of Daniel 8:14. The result is 1843.

History has demonstrated conclusively that Miller was wrong. And Miller was wise enough to admit it, although he could detect no error in his calculations. But when Edson revealed that "the sanctuary to be cleansed is in heaven," and Crozier found him a proof text in Hebrews 8:1, 2, Mrs. White canonized the discovery.[21] It does behoove us, however, since history must needs be silent on such a claim, to investigate whether this fanciful rendering is made out of whole cloth like the alleged ascension robes of the Adventists.

First, then, let us note what Hebrews 8:1, 2 has to say: ". . . we have such a high priest, one who is seated at the right hand of the throne of the Majesty in heaven, a minister in the sanctuary and the true tent which is set up not by man but by the Lord." It does surely indicate that there is a heavenly sanctuary, and that Christ is its priest. But it also indicates that He has already sat down (presumably, having completed His work of atonement). It is clearly taught in Scripture that Christ cried out on the cross, "It is finished"; that the veil separating the Holy Place from the Holy of Holies tore from top to bottom (indicating that Christ made possible a new way of access to the throne of God); and that Jesus fulfilled all the Old Testament prophecies and types of atonement, making further sacrifices unnecessary. Had the Adventists not been driven by despair and disappointment, they probably would not have denied all these things.

According to Adventists, now that Christ has entered the heavenly sanctuary, He makes an "investigative judgment," to use Mrs. White's term; that is, He investigates the professed believers to see who are really in the faith. When this is completed, He will return to the world. At His return, the righteous who are living will be translated to heaven, and the righteous dead will be resurrected and taken to the same place. There they will spend the millennium—and not on the earth. The earth will be desolate during this whole period. But, meanwhile, the punishment of the wicked will be determined. After this unique millennium, Christ will return to the earth with the righteous "where eternity will be spent."[22] Satan and the wicked will be annihilated.

---

[21] Loughborough, *The Great Second Advent Movement*, p. 192.
[22] Clark, *The Small Sects in America*, 2nd edition, p. 42.

2 Doctrines of the Seventh-day Adventists

Doctrine of the Bible

The Bible is inspired, but not verbally and infallibly so. The prophetess, Mrs. Ellen G. White, apparently regarded her interpretations on a par with the Bible. "When I send you a testimony of warning and reproof, many of you declare it to be merely the opinion of Sister White. You have thereby insulted the Spirit of God" (Ellen G. White, *Testimonies,* Vol. V, pp. 661, 664). The Seventh-day Adventists have acknowledged her authority and continue to maintain it today, as this official statement of the General Conference reported in the Seventh-day Adventist Journal, *The Advent Review and Herald,* shows: "Seventh-Day Adventists hold that Ellen G. White performed the work of a true prophet during the seventy years of her public ministry. . . . As Samuel was a prophet . . . as Jeremiah was a prophet . . . as John the Baptist. . . , so we believe that Mrs. White was a prophet to the church of Christ today" (Oct. 4, 1928). Such a statement places Mrs. White in the category with the recognized inspired agents of the Bible; the following does the same by condemning a person who accepted some parts of her *Testimonies* and not others with these words: "This is precisely the attitude taken by the 'higher critics' toward the Bible. They single out certain parts of the Bible and assert that these are not inspired. But no more subtle nor effective method can be employed than this to break down all faith in all inspired writings. . . . The Ellen G. White books are a tower of spiritual power . . . a guiding light to the Adventist people" (*The Advent Review and Herald,* April 4, 1957). T. E. Rabok summarized the whole matter: "The Bible is not verbally inspired; and neither are the writings of Ellen G. White" (*BHP,* p. 194)—yet both are inspired. The Articles of Faith affirm the Bible to be the "unerring rule of *faith and practice" (1957 Yearbook,* p. 4, italics mine).

Doctrine of God

God is tri-personal and His essential attribute is love. "It is the supreme relation between Himself and all created life—yes, the supreme relation between the Persons of the ever-blessed Trinity" (A. S. Maxwell, *Your Friends the Adventists,* p. 18). Only God is immortal, according to the Adventists (Ochat, *TB,* p. 42).

Doctrine of Man

The Seventh-day Adventists differ very little from most Protestant churches "in their teaching concerning the nature of man." This is clear from the official statement: "Mortal man possesses a nature inherently sinful and dying. Eternal life is the gift of God through faith in Christ" (*1957 Yearbook,* p. 4). Nevertheless, one writer (Ochat) says: "If man had never sinned, he would have lived eternally." This seems in keeping with Mrs. White's conception that "his [man's] nature was in harmony with the will of God. His mind was capable of comprehending divine things. His affections were pure; his appetites and passions were under the control of reason. He was holy and happy in bearing the image of God, and in perfect obedience to his will" (*Patriarchs and Prophets,* p. 45). She goes further, saying: "So long as they [Adam and Eve] remained loyal to the divine law, their capacity to know, to enjoy, to love, would continually increase" (ibid., p. 51). The first parents had "no bias toward evil" (p. 49), but nevertheless did have a "desire for self-indulgence, the fatal passion" (p. 48). Man's very freedom required his ability to transgress God's commands and this he did. Though Adam was holy and growing in holiness, still "it was *possible* [italics mine] for Adam, before the fall, to form a righteous character. . ." (Ellen G. White, *Steps to Christ,* p. 65).

Doctrine of Sin

A clear doctrine of the imputation of Adam's guilt is not to be found in Seventh-day Adventist teaching. Mrs. White says that Adam could have formed a righteous character, "But he failed to do this, and because of his sin our natures are fallen, and we cannot make ourselves righteous" (*SC,* p. 65). "The unaided human will has no real power to resist and overcome evil" (Ellen G. White, *Ministry of Healing,* p. 429). The infinite price necessary for redemption shows that sin is a "tremendous evil." In *Steps to Christ* (p. 19), the prophetess says: "But through disobedience, his [man's] powers were perverted, and selfishness took the place of love." Sin, however, is not considered to be totally enslaving; the soul can and "must submit to God" (*SC,* p. 46). At the same time, "The unaided human will has no real power to resist and overcome evil" (*Ministry of Healing,* p. 429). There is apparently an exception in the case of the sin of unbelief, for belief may and must precede regeneration. This implies fallen man's ability to believe.

Doctrine of Christ

"Jesus Christ is very God, being of the same nature and essence as the Eternal Father" (*1957 Yearbook,* p. 4). Deviating from Christian orthodoxy, the Adventists teach that Christ took a polluted human nature: "In His humanity Christ partook of our sinful, fallen nature. If not, then He was not 'made like unto His Brethren,' was not 'in all points tempted like as we are,' did not overcome as we have to overcome, and is not therefore, the complete and perfect Saviour man needs and must have to be saved" (*Bible Readings for the Home Circle*, 1915 ed., p. 115). "Our Saviour took humanity, with all its liabilities. He took the nature of man, with the possibility of yielding to temptation" (Ellen G. White, *The Desire of Ages*, p. 117). Some writers believe that the Adventists no longer hold this doctrine of the Incarnation. Their latest official statement neither affirms nor denies it: "While retaining His divine nature He took upon Himself the nature of the human family, lived on the earth as a man, exemplified in His life as our Example the principles of righteousness . . ." (*1957 Yearbook*, p. 4). The handling of the classical text on this point, Heb. 4:15, in the *Seventh-day Adventist Bible Commentary* is significant. With reference to Christ's being tempted "in all points," the *Commentary* says: "In some mysterious way that we cannot understand, our Lord experienced the full weight of every conceivable temptation the 'prince of this world' (John 12:31) could press upon Him, but without in the least degree, even by a thought, responding to any of them." Christ's being "without sin" is explained thus: "Herein lies the unfathomable mystery of the perfect life of our Saviour. For the first time human nature was led to victory over its natural tendency to sin." This last statement assumes that Christ possessed a "natural tendency to sin," which He conquered.

Doctrine of Redemption

Though God is just, He has mercifully provided a way of salvation through Christ. All have an opportunity to be saved. Those who reject Christ are not damned but annihilated. Those who do believe receive the greater benefit of reconciliation. The Adventist theory of the atonement is as follows: (1) Christ who lived "in blameless obedience to His own eternal law of righteousness offered up a complete, perfect, and all-sufficient sacrifice for the sins of men" (A. S. Maxwell, *Your Friends the Adventists*, p. 19). This was not the atonement, however; for, say the Adventists, "we dissent from the view that the atonement was made upon the cross" (*Fundamental Principles*, p. 2). (2) In 1844, "attended by heavenly angels, our great High Priest enters the Holy of Holies . . . to there make an atonement for all who are shown to be entitled to his benefits" (Ellen G. White, *The Great Controversy*, p. 308). This is Mrs. White's reference to the "investigative judgment" which Christ is thought to have made in the Holy of Holies in heaven. (3) "Before He [Christ] takes His throne as King, He will make the great atonement . . . and their sins will be blotted out" (*FP*). The completion of the atonement comes when Christ, emerging from the Holy of Holies, lays the sins of those who have been found to be true believers upon Azazel (or Satan), who carries away the sins of the world into the wilderness.

The Seventh-day Adventists (who are not especially articulate on this point) consider justification to be an infused, rather than imputed, righteousness. As Mayer observes, "Faith takes hold of Christ's divine power inducting the believing into the covenant relationship where the Law of God is written on his heart, and through the enabling power of the indwelling Christ his life is brought into conformity with the divine precepts" (*Religious Bodies of America,* p. 435). Though often charged with legalism, the Seventh-day Adventists insist that salvation is by faith in Christ and not based on the works of the law, though those are always present. They attempt to avoid both antinomianism and legalism.

With the power of Christ within, the Seventh-day Adventist is to work out his sanctification by strict conformity to the law of God. The law as given in the Old Testament remains largely unchanged for the Adventist. He believes that the sixth commandment requires abstinence from war, tobacco, alcohol, and other detrimental social or personal practices. "The Seventh-day Adventists make the use of intoxicants and tobacco in any form the ground for exclusion from church fellowship" (R. S. Howells, *His Many Mansions,* p. 36). By far the greatest concern is with the fourth commandment. "Sabbath" in the commandment is taken to mean Saturday rather than the day of rest. It is therefore taught that the holy day could never be changed to another day in the week without overthrowing the fourth commandment. Saturday Sabbath was founded at the creation and Adam's fall was caused by his violation of it, according to some Adventist interpretations of Hosea 6:7. This command is the center of the whole law. "In support of this assertion they say that of 497 words which make the Decalog in the English form (AV) the word 'is' of the Sabbath Commandment ('This *is* the Sabbath of the Lord') is the 249th word, or exactly in the center of the Decalog" (Carlyle B. Haynes, *The Christian Sabbath,* p. 34). Sunday observance is the mark of the beast referred to in Revelation 16:2, which mark is on the harlot of Babylon according to Revelation 14 (cf. White, *The Great Controversy,* 1911 ed., p. 449). Sunday worship was, according to the Prophets, the abomination which had to be cleansed from the Holy of Holies when Christ entered in 1844. The Evangelist D. E. Venden regarded Sunday worship as "the unpardonable sin" (cf. Van Baalen, *The Chaos of Cults,* p. 188).

Doctrine of the Church

The general Christian interpretation of the New Testament church in relation to the Old Testament Israel is that it is the same in "substance" (all are believers in the mercy of God) and different only in "accidents" (the mode of worship, etc.). The Adventists tend to reject even the modal differences between the Old Testament and the New Testament church. Thus, the very day of worship must not be changed; dietary laws are still in force; Jerusalem is still the proper center of worship; the payment of the tithe is required; circumcision and the Passover are still observed (cf. Paul Scheurlen, *Die Sekten der Gegenwart*, p. 20).

A tendency to separate from professing Christendom, since she is the harlot of Babylon with the mark of the beast, was to be anticipated. Separation occurred in spite of the advice of the original leader of the movement, William Miller (*Signs of the Times*, Jan. 31, 1844, p. 196). "S.D.A. requires for baptism a confession that the S.D.A. Church 'is the remnant Church' (excluding all others!)" (Van Baalen, *CC*, p. 188). The papacy is Anti-Christ (Dan. 7:25), the first beast of Revelation. Since "followers of Christ will be led to abstain from all intoxicating drinks, tobacco, and other narcotics, and to avoid body and soul defiling habit and practice," vast masses of professing Christians are implicitly unchurched. This principle does not appear to prevent cooperation with some other denominations.

The organization of the Seventh-day Adventists is rather Baptistic. A group of believers may form a local, autonomous congregation which is supervised by one or more elders. Local congregations join to form larger district unions. A General Conference is convened quadrennially. Seventh-day Adventists are Baptistic not only in autonomous, congregational government but in their practice of baptism of adults only and that by immersion. Also practiced at their quarterly meetings is the rite of foot-washing (Howells, *His Many Mansions*, pp. 35f.; *Questions on Doctrine*, p. 24).

Doctrine of the Future

(1) Christ entered into the heavenly Holy of Holies. William Miller, on the basis of Daniel 8:14 (interpreting 2300 days as 2300 years), concluded that 2300 years were to elapse prior to the return of Christ. But 2300 years from what date? Miller thought it was 457 B.C. (*AD*, chap. II) from which the following calculation was made:

$$- \ 457 \ \text{B.C.}$$
$$+2300 \ \text{years}$$
$$+\text{A.D.} \ 1843 \ \text{the date of the return.}$$

Later he modified his calculation to 1844, then repudiated the whole scheme when Christ did not return. The Seventh-day Adventists adopted the view that Christ did come, but not to earth — rather to the heavenly Holy of Holies to purify it and instigate the Investigative Judgment. (2) Investigative Judgment. Christ entered the heavenly Holy of Holies and began the searching of hearts to see who were true

Christians. "This work of judgment in the heavenly sanctuary began in 1844. Its completion will close human probation" (*1975 Yearbook,* p. 5). (3) Christ will come out of the Holy of Holies and lay the guilt of His people on Azazel. (4) Imminently He will come to the earth to annihilate the wicked and resurrect His people, living and dead (the souls sleep at death until this resurrection [*Fundamental Principles,* p. 12]). He will take them with Him to heaven for the millennium, leaving Satan on the desolate earth. (5) Christ will return to earth to accomplish three purposes: a. Destroy Satan; b. Purify the earth by fire (II Peter 3:10); c. Live with His resurrected saints (the 144,000) on the regenerated earth for eternity.

3 Terms Frequently Used by the Seventh-day Adventists

Annihilation: The doctrine that unbelievers will not be eternally punished, but will be destroyed.

Armageddon: Impending battle in Palestine between the hosts of Christ and Antichrist, which will issue in the destruction of the latter.

Azazel: The name of the scapegoat used in the sacrifice on the day of atonement. Mrs. White taught that Azazel was a type of Satan, who was the scapegoat for the sins of God's people.

Great Controversy; Mrs. White's most basic writing, describing the great historic struggle between God and the devil.

Investigative Judgment: Refers to the activity of Christ, which began in 1844 when He entered the Holy of Holies. Until His second advent, He will examine the hearts of all professing Christians to ascertain their sincerity.

Liberty: A magazine expressing Adventist principles of the Sabbath and advocating separation of church and state.

Midnight Cry: The announcement which immediately precedes the return of Christ; the term is based on the parable of the ten virgins (Matt. 25:1-13).

Millennium: The coming visible reign of Christ on earth during which an effective enforced peace will prevail and evangelization will be accelerated.

Patriarchs and Prophets: One of the more important of the many writings of Mrs. Mary Ellen White.

Signs of the Times: An Adventist periodical.

Soul-sleep: At death, the soul of the Christian passes into a state of unconsciousness until the return of Christ.

2300: "Unto two thousand and three hundred days; then shall the sanctuary be cleansed" (Dan. 8:14). This is taken to mean 2300 years from the defiling of the temple in 457 B.C.:

$$- \ 457 \ \text{B.C.}$$
$$\underline{+2300} \ \text{years}$$
$$\text{A.D. } 1843$$

1843, therefore, was the date calculated by William Miller to be the time of Christ's return. Later he figured it at 1844. Still later, the movement adopted Mary Ellen White's interpretation that Christ did return in 1844, but not to earth—instead, He entered the heavenly Holy of Holies to present the blood of the atonement.

4 For Further Reading

Andross, Mrs. Matilda. *Story of the Adventist Message.* Washington, D.C.: Review and Herald Publishing Co., n.d.

Bible Readings for the Home: A Topical Study in Question and Answer Form. Washington, D.C.: Review and Herald Publishing Co., 1947.

Bliss, Sylvester. *Memoirs of William Miller, Generally Known as a Lecturer on the Prophecies, and the Second Coming of Christ.* 1853. Reprint. New York: AMS Press, n.d.

Froom, LeRoy Edwin. *The Prophetic Faith of Our Fathers.* 4 vols. Washington, D.C.: Review and Herald Publishing Co., 1950.

_____. "Seventh-Day Adventists." In *The American Church of the Protestant Heritage,* edited by Vergilius T. Ferm. 1953. Reprint. Westport, Conn.: Greenwood Press, Inc., n.d.

Hoekema, Anthony A. *Seventh-day Adventism.* Grand Rapids: Wm. B. Eerdmans Publishing Co., 1974.

Lewis, Gordon. *The Bible, the Christian, and Seventh-day Adventists.* Nutley, N.J.: Presbyterian & Reformed Publishing Co., 1966.

_____. *Confronting the Cults.* Nutley, N.J.: Presbyterian & Reformed Publishing Co., 1966.

Lindsell, Harold. "What of Seventh-day Adventism?" *Christianity Today,* March 31, 1958 and April 14, 1958.

Loughborough, J. N. *The Great Second Advent Movement, Its Rise and Progress.* 1905. Reprint. New York: Arno Press, n.d.

Martin, Walter R. *The Truth About Seventh-day Adventism.* Grand Rapids: Zondervan Publishing House, 1960.

_____. *The Kingdom of the Cults.* Grand Rapids: Zondervan Publishing House, 1965.

Nichol, Francis D. "The Growth of the Millerite Legend." *Church History,* vol. 21, no. 4 (1952), pp. 296 ff.

_____. *The Midnight Cry. A Defense of the Character and Conduct of William Miller and the Millerites, Who Mistakenly Believed that the Second Coming of Christ Would Take Place in the Year 1844.* 1944. Reprint. New York: AMS Press, n.d.

Olsen, M. Ellsworth. *A History of the Origin and Progress of Seventh-Day Adventists.* 1925. Reprint. New York: AMS Press, n.d.

Sears, Clara Endicott. *Days of Delusion.* New York: Houghton Mifflin Co., 1924.

Seventh-Day Adventists Answer Questions on Doctrine. Washington, D.C.: Review and Herald Publishing Co., 1957.

Smith, Uriah. *The Prophecies of Daniel and the Revelation.* Nashville: Southern Publishing Association, 1949.

Talbot, Louis T. *What's Wrong with Seventh-Day Adventism?* Findlay, Ohio: Dunham Publishing Co., 1956.

White, Ellen G. *The Desire of Ages; the Conflict of the Ages Illustrated in the Life of Christianity.* Mountain View, Calif.: Pacific Press Publishing Assn., 1940.

5 Summary of Traditional Christian Doctrines

In the following chapter we present views which are held by the church without exception (unless so indicated). There are three main branches of the catholic (universal) church: Protestant, Eastern Orthodox, and Roman Catholic. These have differences among them, but there is a remarkable consensus of viewpoint on the basic structure of Christian doctrine. This fact is justification for use of the term "the catholic church." We have chosen quotations from official creeds of these branches to illustrate the various doctrines.

Doctrine of the Bible

The catholic church believes the sixty-six books of the Old Testament and New Testament to be the plenarily inspired Word of God. The Roman Church adds to this number some of the apocrypha. The Roman and Eastern Orthodox churches seem to give ecclesiastical tradition virtually equal authority with Scripture. The Protestant churches, however, hold to *sola scriptura*. Thus, the Lutheran Formula of Concord affirms: "We believe, confess, and teach that the only rule and norm, according to which all dogmas and all doctors ought to be esteemed and judged, is no other whatever than the prophetic and apostolic writings both of the Old and of the New Testament." The French Confession of Faith says of the Bible that "inasmuch as it is the rule of all truth, containing all that is necessary for the service of God and for our salvation, it is not lawful for men, nor even for angels, to add to it, to take away from it, or to change it." The American Revision of the Thirty-Nine Articles of the Church of England states: "Holy Scripture containeth all things necessary to salvation: so that whatsoever is not read therein, nor may be proved thereby, is not to be required of any man, that it should be believed as an article of the Faith, or be thought requisite *or* necessary to salvation."

Doctrine of God

The Athanasian Creed, accepted as an ecumenical creed by all branches of the church, reads: ". . . we worship one God in Trinity, and Trinity in Unity; Neither confounding the Persons, nor dividing the Substance [Essence]. For there is one Person of the Father, another of the Son, and another of the Holy Ghost. But the Godhead of the Father, of the Son, and of the Holy Ghost is all one, the Glory equal, the Majesty co-eternal. Such as the Father is, such is the Son, and such is the Holy Ghost. The Father uncreate, the Son uncreate, and the Holy Ghost uncreate. The Father incomprehensible [unlimited], the Son incomprehensible [unlimited], and the Holy Ghost incomprehensible [unlimited or infinite]. The Father eternal, the Son eternal, and the Holy Ghost eternal. And yet they are not three eternals, but one eternal. . . . So the Father is God, the Son is God, and the Holy Ghost is God. And yet they are not three Gods, but one God. . . . the Unity in Trinity and the Trinity in Unity is to be worshiped." The Westminster Shorter Catechism teaches: "There are three persons in the Godhead: the Father, the Son, and the Holy Ghost; and these three are one God, the same in substance, equal in power and glory."

Doctrine of Man

Again we may use the Westminster Shorter Catechism, for it expresses what all catholic churches believe about man. "God created man, male and female, after his own image, in knowledge, righteousness, and holiness, with dominion over the creatures."

Doctrine of Sin

The Roman Catholic statement made at the Council of Trent contains a catholic affirmation: ". . . Adam, when he had transgressed the commandment of God in Paradise, immediately lost the holiness and justice wherein he had been constituted; and . . . he incurred, through the offense of that prevarication, the wrath and indignation of God, and consequently death, with which God had previously threatened him, and, together with death, captivity under his power who thenceforth *had the empire of death, that is to say, the devil,* and that the entire Adam, through that offense of prevarication, was changed, in body and soul, for the worse. . . . this sin of Adam . . . [is] transfused into all by propagation, not by imitation. . . ." All catholic churches say at least this much; some, such as the Reformed, make more of the consequences of the Fall.

Doctrine of Christ

We may use the historic confession of the Council of Chalcedon (A.D. 451), for this has been recognized through the ages by all branches of orthodox Christendom as a true statement concerning the person of Jesus Christ. ". . . our Lord Jesus Christ, the same perfect in Godhead and also perfect in manhood; truly God and truly man, of a reasonable [rational] soul and body; consubstantial [coessential] with the Father according to the Godhead, and consubstantial with us according to the Manhood; in all things like unto us, without sin;

begotten before all ages of the Father according to the Godhead, and
in these latter days, for us and for our salvation, born of the Virgin
Mary, the Mother of God, according to the Manhood; one and the
same Christ, Son, Lord, Only-begotten, to be acknowledged in two
natures, *inconfusedly, unchangeably, indivisibly, inseparably;* the dis-
tinction of natures being by no means taken away by the union, but
rather the property of each nature being preserved, and concurring in
one Person and one Subsistence, not parted or divided into two
persons, but one and the same Son, and only begotten, God the Word,
the Lord Jesus Christ. . . ."

We note that the expression, "Mary, the Mother of God," is a
genuinely catholic expression. It does not mean that Mary was the
genetrix of God, but that the human nature which was begotten in her
womb was united with the eternal Son of God. So Mary was the
mother of the child who was God; i.e., the mother of God.

Doctrine of Redemption

The satisfaction view of the atonement is the truly classic view of
the catholic church. This could be shown from Protestant, Roman, or
Eastern Orthodox creeds. We will show it by a citation from "The
Longer Catechism" of the Eastern Orthodox Church: "Therefore as in
Adam we had fallen under sin, the curse, and death, so we are deliv-
ered from sin, the curse, and death in Jesus Christ. His voluntary
suffering and death on the cross for us, being of infinite value and
merit, as the death of one sinless, God and man in one person, is both
a perfect satisfaction to the justice of God, which had condemned us
for sin to death, and a fund of infinite merit, which has obtained him
the right, without prejudice to justice, to give us sinners pardon of our
sins, and grace to have victory over sin and death."

There is a great difference among the three divisions of Christendom concerning the appropriation of this redemption achieved by
Christ. The Protestant churches teach that it is by faith alone; the
other branches incline to the view that it is by faith and works, or by
faith considered as the beginning of works.

All branches of the church teach that the Christian has an obligation to endeavor to keep the moral law of God and that a person who
does not do so is a reprobate. There is a doctrine in the Roman
Church which is inconsistent with this, but nevertheless she teaches
the above explicitly.

Doctrine of the Church

The Westminster Confession of Faith contains a definition of the
church shared by all bodies of Christendom which accept the notion
of the invisibility of the church. "The catholic or universal Church,
which is invisible, consists of the whole number of the elect, that have

been, are, or shall be gathered into one, under Christ the head thereof; and is the spouse, the body, the fullness of Him that filleth all in all. The visible Church, which is also catholic or universal under the gospel (not confined to one nation, as before under the law), consists of all those, throughout the world, that profess the true religion, and of their children, and is the kingdom of the Lord Jesus Christ, the house and family of God, out of which there is no ordinary possibility of salvation."

Doctrine of the Future

While there has been less defining of the doctrine of the future by the catholic church than has been true of other doctrines, what has been stated is unanimously affirmed. All branches of Christendom are agreed that there is a place of eternal felicity, called heaven, where redeemed men and unfallen angels dwell in the gracious presence of God. It is also taught that there is a place of eternal misery, called hell, where all unredeemed men and fallen angels dwell in the wrathful presence of God. The Roman Catholic Church maintains, in addition, the existence of purgatory, the *limbus patrum,* and the *limbus infantum.* Universal salvation has been taught by various individuals, but no church recognized by catholic Christianity has affirmed it.

6 Brief Definitions of the Sects

Seventh-day Adventism teaches that salvation is attained by faith in the atonement made by Christ in 1844. This faith must be expressed in obedience to the ethical teachings of the Bible (including the law of the Saturday Sabbath) and in acceptance of the doctrinal teachings of the Bible (including the imminent premillennial return of Christ).

Jehovah's Witnesses claim to be the only consistent Bible students. They find the vindication of Jehovah to be the fundamental aim of history. This vindication is accomplished by the atonement of the first-born creature, Jesus, and expressed by the witnessing to an impending Armageddon. At this battle Jehovah and His Witnesses will be vindicated and the final consummation of things will begin.

Mormonism is built on a revelation subsequent to the Bible, called the *Book of Mormon*. According to this book, the church is to be reorganized on the basis of a creed which teaches a plurality of created gods, repudiates justification by faith, and teaches salvation achieved by the merit of obeying divine laws.

Christian Science is a formula for health and wealth by right thinking, but its thinking denies the reality of poverty and sickness.

CHART OF COMPARATIVE DOCTRINES

	Traditional Christian	Seventh-day Adventism	Jehovah's Witnesses	Mormonism	Christian Science
Bible	Verbally inspired	Reluctant to affirm verbal inspiration; vague about status of Mrs. White	Verbally inspired	Inspired Bible and Book of Mormon	Bible inspired and *Science and Health* is its inspired interpretation
God	Three Persons in one Essence	Approximately traditional Christian view	Uni-personal	Polytheism	Impersonal and pantheistic
Man	Body-soul created good	Body-soul creature, created neutral or with inclination to evil	Body. Soul not distinguishable from body	Pre-existent soul takes body at birth in this world	Soul only; body is an illusion
Sin	Result of Adam's Disobedience; corruption of nature and action	No clear doctrine of imputation of Adam's sin; man now polluted	Adam's sin brought liability to temporal death	It was necessary for Adam to sin. This brought mortality without guilt	"There is no sin" — it is illusion
Christ	One divine person in two distinct natures (divine-human)	Like traditional view but represents human nature as having tendency to sin	First-born creature; changed into man at birth in this world	Called creator but only pre-existent spirit who took body at incarnation	Christ is a divine idea; Jesus is mere human
Redemption	Faith in atonement as expressed by holy life	Believing in atonement made in heaven plus holy living including observance of Saturday Sabbath	Christ's ransom gives man chance to earn salvation	Atonement gives man chance to earn salvation	Salvation by casting out idea of sin
Church	Mystical union of all true believers, visable union of all professed believers	Seems to regard itself as true remnant church	Traditional church rejected 144,000 Witnesses make up church	Other churches apostate; efficient hierarchical organization	A denomination like Protestant, Roman Catholic, and Jewish
Future	Eternal heaven, eternal hell, temporary purgatory (R.C.)	Annihilation of wicked; millennium in heaven and eternity on new earth	Earthly millennium during which final probation leading to annihilation or eternal life	Pre-millennial reign at Independence, Mo.; tends toward universal salvation	Universal salvation in future when idea of sin gradually dies